TONGUES TIED TO ANCHORS

Tongues Tied To Anchors

By Laurence Wilhelm Lillvik

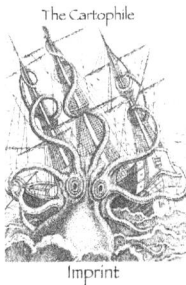

The Cartophile

Imprint

Tongues Tied To Anchors by Laurence Wilhelm Lillvik
ISBN 978-0-9824674-1-1

All poems written in 2009 except
"The Soft Lust of Extinction" which appeared in *Vapor/Strains*.
"Honey Mead" which appeared in *Dogmatika*,
and "Ante Meridiem."

For Jennie.

Contents:

Tongues Tied To Anchors

DIY

She applied bacon
Grease to her pressure
Points, lay naked in
The muddy pond, and
Waited for the crawdads.

I Blame The Antihistamines

Dawn has nested

Upon our calamari

Scribbles. We are

Catching on, and on

To the drone-kissed

Cliffs we sail.

Sirens dislodge them—

Selves from monoliths,

Swim beside us, tongues-

Tied to our anchors.

Beatrice, release the

Alchemists from your

Lover's inferno, for

Little clock remains,

And we're poor match

For this beastly scrum.

Cape Disappointment

Moored to this
Bird-shit rock,
In this sea-sick fog,
I can't see the stars,
So as the seals bark-
I reach for my gin-jar.

The Soft Lust Of Extinction

Be it a bleak stain as observable and
Fly-specked as a copyrite infringement,
A song of musk-ox yet less erudite, near
Malleable upon billboards. This patience,

Bitch-meandering thru coppertop hosannas,
Small-speakered tweet above fir-tipped
Roofscape, tar-topping the broadlight,
Will be beaten before the beak-pecked

Hatch of eggshell. The curtaining
Aspect of her eye soothes only the
Snowpacked loss and inward flight
Of the dodo. Hope entrenched in scar.

Empire Building

Her client, the imperialist, woke jealous
Of his neighbor's wind chimes. He found
Her business card used as a bookmark in
"A History of Land Mines." He lived next

To a Latino family who sold warm Budweiser
To crack heads and college kids after hours.
She urged her client to research the climate
And name his moods like the weather bureau

Names tropical storms. She said imperialism
Grows where crops fail and then works its
Way to the equator. He said he was pleased
because quinine was such an excellent flavor

Agent. She's taken to wearing a pith helmet
To their bi-weekly sessions. Yesterday it was
Their bird bath, he said. She smiled and rubbed
A lime on the edge of their highball glasses.

No Winter's Captive

Somewhere in

That drawer lies a

Logic as formidable as a lock-

Pick. Take

That chap with the

Yankee tarnish,

Who else could have escaped

That pen

With no

More than a few

Barbed-wire abrasions?

(That wallet once gifted

With a card inside asking me

To forgive the scars and

Irregularities of the bovine

Skin, for they occurred

Naturally, when the cows

Rub against

That razor wire.)

That mound of leaves irritates

My view, now hidden is the

Belly of

That malingering gamine.

She tickles the wrist-ropes,
Weakening shadows, elongated

By impatient flickers and flare-ups,
That fire hazard lifestyle making
Me itch.

What, Honey?

Wendy, when you read to
Me, when you *really* fucking
Read to me, all I can hear
Is the goddamn buzzing of

Government-sponsored bee-
Keepers, they're everywhere
Wendy. Without bees our
Food is gone, is what they're

Saying at the co-op, except for
Those meat tubes that just
Eat and eliminate, I've seen
Drawings, Wendy, a mouth

And an anus, and a bunch
Of muscle-fiber we can chow
On, and ethics aside it's a little
Nasty. Now, I would have never

Guessed my ghosts would want
To join us in your quonset hut,
But every night I can hear Henry
Miller pissing in a whore's bidet.

Always Parsimonious

Always parsimonious,

I watched you get an

Idea, then snatch

The lightbulb,

To screw into a rusty projector.

You decorate the wall,

Of the room in which

We've never set foot,

With a moldy slide-show.

A Poem For Patricia Highsmith

His

Biography

Was

Published

A

Fortnight

Before

He

Had

Seen

Patricia's

Breasts

Bared

In

A

Photograph,

So

The

Events

That

Transpired

Thereafter

Required

A

Novella-

Length

Epilogue

Be

Tacked

Onto

The

Later

Editions.

Owl

A macrame owl,

And all it portends,

Hangs in the basement.

Cleaning Batshit From A Villainous Nest

No fist, no framework, her
Lipstick inappropriate, her
Vestments: spider-silk.
"Nature's kevlar,"

I whispered

To the boom operator.
She was lit from below and
The poachers wrung their
Mitts, and the spume now

Did spill, uncanny and
Damned, over the sides of
The vile aquariums. The
Alternative weeklies have

Taken to abusing such
Phrases as "Bat Shit Crazy"
Though The Judge knows
That guano can cauterize

  a mountainside.

Colt's Neck, NJ, 1989

When you inhaled
The third world dis-
Appeared and you

Dropped the roach
Onto the iced pond.

Hungry ghosts howled
And skirted the birch-
Edged perimeter.

Back inside we
Shot billiards to the
Sabbath soundtrack.

Death Valley '09

And the conversation,
Once again, drifted
To Bobby Beausoleil.

A restrictive lip-ring
On a lisping hipster
Glints as she whispers
Mischievous hints.

Fealty

Little girl, barking

Manifestos, your

Father swallowed

Cities. Your fealty,

However cluttered,

To this miserable

Osmosis, is no act

Of mercy. Now he

Vomits from the

Aftertaste- metal,

Concrete, and skin.

But let's not kid

Ourselves, for we

Are paid to remain

Uncalcified and un-

Solvent.

Van Gogh

Window Shade

How could you
Cut off the top
Of this painting?
He asked. But
It's just a little
Piece of the sky,
She replied.

An Uneasy Proximity

Eastward, over the mountains
A spell, and below the soil,
Let me tell you. Three feet
Beneath, and the acreage, oh-

It makes me tremble. A mush-
Room, my friend, the world's
Largest organism. Now, on
A separate threaded thought,

Yesterday I coughed, while
Listening to a recording four
Decades old, and as soon as
I coughed, someone in the

Background of the recording,
(A field recording, dig, in a
Cafe, or something) coughed.
Now I'm not talking about a

Super-organism, an ant colony
Or something. So I rewound the
Tape to make sure this person
In the background didn't cough

First, leading me on, as such,
Causation, like in a library,
Or movie theatre, cough as
Contagion. 16,000 football

Fields needed to contain this
Subterranean Fungi, just over
The Cascades. No fear of this
Giant organism is irrational.

Mentioning

In the second
Translation -there
In eroded Palmer

Method, in a
Page-pile, a
Hoard-stack-

(He was dragon-
Greedy for her
Words, I suppose)

She mentions the
Mumbling yegg.

Mausoleum

I'd almost always apologize
When they asked
How or what.

It is no coincidence, we whispered
Until I felt the piss trickle down my
Pajama leg.

No one we know is in a mausoleum,
No one can hold on to the chalk, but
We were lucky to clap the erasers.

Dream Battery

Not Eveready but percussion,

I dream bash nuns and

Greasy interlopers and I've seen

Enough moving pictures to know

To never let up until their

Heads stain the pavement.

Merge. Flatten the image like

Photoshop layers. While my

Strikes are invariably preemptive,

Be it by bat or block of cinder, I

Never do rest easy knowing

Justice has been served.

Breakfast Poem

EVERY slick increment of
TIME, the begrudging encumbrances of morning -
YOU with the concrete sinus
START by fidgeting and forcing the smile,
AN antidote to the mission statements-
ASH pallor pale wan until the
TRAY arrives and we hydrate, the
FIRE of the dreams now dulling,
IN short bursts of breath we arrive, as
THE facsimile of lives, day pigeons in the
DINER, "rats with wings" the quip I quote, tho I
HAVE no theories re: it's attribution, so
A tour bus winces past the window, and you feign
PANIC, as she wipes the Specials Board clean -
ATTACK your omelette with gusto.

Sprung Poem

And this I

know you

sketch the

shrubs I

piss I drink

a sip you

sketch the

fence I climb

I balance I do

not want to I

do not want

to trip.

(I fashion a

lasso from

Claudia

Cardinale's

eye lashes

while humming

an unwritten

funeral mass)

I leap a spell

you sketch

my cast I break

the lock you

sketch the lid

you sketch the
hasp the chest
is full I tumble
back our fortune's
made our fortune's
made.

Ponder The Architect

You shouldn't shiver when you
Ponder the architect, however,

You should think of the trees,
On either side of the boulevard,
That touch above the cars.

His missives, his mistresses.

Ante Meridiem

The angernaut manipulates
Vitriolic polymers while

Just outside his door she
Vacuums up the last crumbs

Of laughter into an oil lamp
To be emptied when the

Crows allow passage to the
Curbside. To shuttle his

Gifts of reason, the angernaut
Travels the synaptic interstates

And prole-funded toll roads,
Avoiding backstreets where

Mongrels of instinct, hole-
Pokers, and taste makers

Costume themselves in
The alchemy of unfettered

Access to the nightmares
Of passers-by.

Ripped Map

Now ponder the cartographer

And all of the fauna who

Interpret the lancing

Of the clumsy troubadour

As a prop for the minstrels,

As a legal challenge.

Isn't this the territory,

Excised from the parchment,

That lines the steamer trunk

In perpetual hock?

Queen Of The Pancakes

To withstand

The unnerving verbiage

Of a

Kettle whistling itself dry

She climbed

Above the selection committee

And

Mounted herself

Upon the

Wood-

Paneled wall,

All the while

Undulating greasily.

Lewis and Clark

An ambition tweaked and flicked
Like an earlobe, like the weather.

He detested the apples.

Though warm enough, the rain was
A threat, they ate their mounts.

Observe his sea-spanked bottom.

Inherent

Deprived of another child
Bride, and universally regarded

As remarkably functionless, due
To permanent state of empathy,

He impregnated the Venus of
Willendorf. Now, dipped in

The sour milk-bath of millennia,
We can argue the angles once

Shrouded by ancestral detractors.
But we won't, will we?

Speculative Beachcombing

Spent the day piling drift wood.

Shaping it into a shelter.

Knowing it couldn't do shit against a real storm.

Watching the skies for a real storm.

Dragging the vinyl cushions stolen from those assholes' patio.

Worrying about the rubbers.

Buying the rubbers and two bottles of DM cough syrup.

Waiting outside the liquor store.

Giving money to the bum.

Drinking four beers in forty-five minutes, half a DM.

Carving the sign into a plywood plank.

"Welcome Back Brandy."

Wondering where the fuck she is.

Honey Mead

It's not as if some dirt adept, harvest-seasoned
And corn-tickled, took off with your tractor, or

A maze of landscape was altered in your absence.
More like your weary focus blurred into a
landfill

Of spectators draped in the colors of
resignation.
Your borrowed focus lures neighbors of

Light into racoonish forays through your passion
Pantry. Paw-prints in marmalade, and gold medal

Flour-tracked across your fussed over blueprints
Demand an action plan, perhaps a board of
advisors.

Mission

Enter the cathedral.

Grow horns. Stampede

Like a riot cop

Past the force-field

Of wilted palm fronds

Until you reconnoiter

The portal beyond the

Velvet ropes. You are

A scout, now wading

Through the gravy

Of the lower planes.

Spying the salvage,

Adrift in the distance

You make buoyant your

Carriage and float past

The saints, long dead,

Though still lipping their

Greetings incoherently.

Daughters of The Insincere

Oh and he found his death.
Oh, and when he found his
Death it was to be by the
Hands of, by the hands of
the Daughters of, of
The Insincere. I saw
You, saw you change,
change your itinerary,
Extend your transit time,
To avoid those certain
Bus routes. I cannot, I
Cannot shoehorn rubies,
Shoehorn rubies by the
Mouthful past your smile.
And those Daughters of,
Daughters of the Insincere
Show no signs of knowing
A thing, a thing such as
The custom of social,
Social reciprocity, tho I
Envy, I really envy their
Pragmatic approach to
The death of the elderly.

Shortage

Dipped ego in abreaction and
Splattered on that brazen web

Spun across the threshold. Did
She, the spider, not notice my

Traffic patterns, or has the
Shortage of flies prompted

Her to troll for more ambitious
Prey? Either way I feel strained

Through a sieve and peppered
About the elemental planes.

Interstellar Space

Drink a bucket
  Of coffee then
Put this on the
  Hi-fi. Try to sit

Still for awhile.
  Allow yourself
To fail. Then
  Flail baby, flail.

Recognitions

Brushing moonlight

From your sleeve,

The fog sculptress

Can see stars from

The bottom of the

Well. When we

Know you, we'll

know if it was a

tragedy. Feel The

weight of the wind-

Chimes, no clocks

To mark the passage

Of someone's shame.

Pounds

Ezra fucks weight

W/

Quid cake beats.

Dawn

I.

Splayed on memory

Foam, ghost-birthing

Our antecedents, in

A trumped up polaroid.

II.

Prayed for diagnoses

In a kayak, circling

Terminal Island, near

Advantageous sunrise.

On The Lam

I dropped
Into your dream
Last night but left a
Scat pile beneath
The Bougainvillea
and fear they're
on my tail.

Ransom

A handful of

Withered nose-

Gays and the

Ransom's been

Paid. Now peel

Me off the page

Of your -1 and

A ½ act play.

Saved

So sacrosanct
is the depression

dug in that cave
deep in the desert,

that your unholy
micturition, upon

contact, vaporizes
and chokes you

with(in) a

pentecostal fog.

Still Life (After Death)

Scattered amid the
Actual wreckage were
Thumbnail sketches of
Inclement intentions,

Skull-sized bilge-pumps
Leaking amniotic fluid,
Eight pounds of lunchmeat,
Mini-cassette recordings

Of axe-handled threats,
Photographs of nail-bitten
Hands with peeling polish,
Probably pre-teen, whiskey

Tumblers full of potting
Soil, and page after page
Of stenographic paper
Smeared with muted lore.

Salve

You disremember the
      filthy brownies,
Halved and quartered
      by necessity,
No salve for situation
      festering, with
Dire lack of levity. But
      I recall it all.

Fallen Poem

I entered toothsome into the
Yard, gave nod to the adherents
Of the cover crop gathered in
A mossy cabal by the legion of

Scarecrows, and heard her exclaim,
"*Everyone's* a fucking enthusiast!"
"More like *shucking* enthusiasts," I
Thought, "how corny they are, tilling

Away on their organ farm." Field's
Edge gave sway to clusters of
Oak and "Beyond that we're on
Our own," was writ into the manual

Of operations. Kidney and liver
Pie, "a seasonal delight," dominated
The menu with an oversized font,
But I was content to sip sangria,

Ogle the hostess, and configure
An exit strategy involving the
Least amount of skin damage. I
Saw a mouser wipe a teardrop with

It's paw and then give lick with swift
Forgetting. But sorrow *here* is subject to
The law of leaves, too soaked-into their
clumped-up mounds to ever blow away.

Forensics

Our ears trying to discern if the
The sound outside is of rain or train,
But at this point does it matter?

We're sipping coffee in a modern
City, once medieval, wishing the
Walls would never let us out,

Wishing the coffee was cognac.

We're wanting to remake "Murder
She Wrote" with explicit violence,
And gratuitous reference to semen,

But nothing "gives us pause" any-
More, and no one steals us flowers
Anymore, and who would swim

That river full of ancient sturgeon?

Modular

She emerged,

Squinting,

From the devil's

Framework,

Panic in a hip

Flask, her share

Of the heating

Bill fleeced, three

Shivers short.

Medicine Man

Like climbing a
cliff to search for
the drowned, the
medicine man got
lost in an eclipse

above the impro-
vised airstrips we
cut with our cane-
knives through the
lending libraries.

Sonnet For Mexico In The Time Of Swine Flu

Well, the dry cleaner is happy as he
Martinizes our snot-sneezed sweater sleeves,
But cruise ships diverted from the palm leaves
Plow North and hope the cliffs provide lee.
The wind blows as bitter as the pig's breath,
And the Northwest coast keeps bleached our pale
skin.
They squeeze Purell onto the hands of kin
Who pace the gangplanks like Ladies MacBeth.
Vaccine complete, we reach Astoria,
Anchor at the mouth of the Columbia,
Graveyard of the Pacific, disembark,
That day's tour regales Lewis and Clark.
The death toll is stable as we re-board,
Sail to Alaska if we can afford.

Malta (For Jennie)

I used to want to give you Malta,

So I could say I gave you Malta,

But I didn't even know you,

Now I do.

I gave you part of Jersey,

But I think you need Savannah.

Beijing, The Badlands, and Memphis,

Were ours for a spell.

A spell we never memorized,

Ever so mythologized,

I swear I'll give you Malta

Someday.